GHOSTS OF THE GARDEN STATE II

GHOSTS OF THE GARDEN STATE II

ISBN 0-9700718-7-6

All photos taken by author unless otherwise noted.

Cover design by: Debra Tremper
                  Six-Penny Graphics
                  Fredericksburg, VA

Back cover cat logo designed by: Glenda Moore
                                  catStuff Graphics

Printed on recycled paper by Sheridan Books. ♻

CONTENTS

According to legend, a ghostly re-enactment of a grisly 1782 massacre occurs nears Barnegat Light every October.

INTRODUCTION

General George Washington directed his coach driver to stop and pick up the little girl he saw struggling to find her way through a blinding blizzard. When the footman was within reach of the girl, she vanished.

Over the decades this petite brown-haired phantom has come to be known as "Amy." Even though her mortal remains are buried in the Old Whitenack Cemetery, her spectral form is seen roaming the area from Basking Ridge to Summit, most often near the train tracks. By all accounts, Amy drowned in a cistern and the reason her earthbound spirit stays behind is to protect children from a similar fate.

Although little is known about the nature of hauntings and why they happen, ghost lore is an American tradition and Amy's tale is only one of many that infiltrate New Jersey's history.

As early as 1894, Garden State ghosts were in the news. Native son Stephen Crane, author of *The Red Badge of Courage* reported: "*a man had better think three times before he openly scorns the legends of the phantoms...if you go into the huckleberry region back of Shark River you had better not scorn the story of the great pirate ship that sails without trouble in twelve inches of water, and has skeletons dangling at the mastheads. Terrible faces peer over the bulwarks, and confound the visions of any who would witness the phantom movements from the shore.*"

1

Just about every New Jersey town can tell a tale of strange phenomena. The state's widespread history predates the American Revolution and makes the region ripe for ghost stories. Revenants from that struggle still roam Princeton University's hallowed halls and Sourland Mountain Reserve's haunted hills.

The Garden State abounds with properties suitable for haunting - some date to the mid-1600s. Since older homes have housed more residents, the odds are greater that a restless spirit will stay on to perturb the place as is the case at the Abbott House in Mays Landing, the Thomas Budd House in Mount Holly, or Morristown's Acorn Hall.

Reputedly, the spirited Jersey Shore harbors hangers-on at Barnegat Light Beach, Ocean City, and Sandy Hook. Apparitions appear at Paterson's baronial acres and even humble settings like Lyndhurst's Little Red Schoolhouse still possess devoted spirits.

Journey back in time across New Jersey's paranormal borderline, beyond the boundary of physical limitations, to haunted places where we can only ponder the phenomenal ghosts that beguile the Garden State.

BARNEGAT LIGHT BEACH
Barnegat Light

Before Scandinavian fishermen settled the tiny seaside community of Barnegat Light and decades before the beam of "Old Barney" would guide sailors to safety, a Revolutionary War event bloodied its sandy beach.

On October 25, 1782, a British ship ran aground near the inlet. Captain Andrew Steelman and his 25 crewmen on the *Alligator* took possession of the wreck and spent the day removing the cargo from the captured vessel.

As night fell, the exhausted men settled down on the dunes for much needed rest. Out of the darkness crept the notorious Pines robber Captain John Bacon and his band of Tory raiders. They massacred nearly all of the unsuspecting men; only five managed to survive the bloody assault.

Bacon became a wanted man and a reward was offered for his capture. In due course, the villain was apprehended at a South Jersey tavern, shot and killed.

A long held legend is that near the site of the historical marker at Barnegat Light that commemorates the gruesome slaughter, ghostly re-enactors replay the gory massacre every October.

3

Pomona Hall provides a "lived-in" environment for its resident ghost.

POMONA HALL
Camden

*I*n 1718 Camden was called "Cooper's Ferry" named after the community's first settler, William Cooper, the Quaker who ran the ferry that transported goods and people to Philadelphia.

Four of the homes constructed by Cooper's descendants still stand in Camden, and Marmaduke Cooper's is supposedly haunted.

Marmaduke's domicile started out as a small wood-framed house. By 1788, the once modest home evolved into Pomona Hall a well-appointed brick mansion. The historic manse is considered "the finest example of a Georgian Style plantation house in New Jersey."

The home is furnished in 18th century fashion and suggests a "lived-in" feel. The dining room table is set and awaits the family. Some surmise they're still there...

Museum staffers encounter cold spots, one of the usual signs of a ghostly presence. The uneasy feeling of someone standing behind them in the restored residence sends chilly sensations down their spine.

High-tech ghost hunting equipment, such as an electro-magnetic field detector, displayed positive readings, and ghostly orbs appeared on film and videotape. The most disconcerting demonstration of all was captured on audiotape - the sobs of a long-ago girl.

Selinda Parry is a "man-hating" ghost who demands attention from beyond the grave.

HUNTERDON ARTS CENTER
Clinton

Clinton is situated at the convergence of Spruce Run and the South Branch of the Raritan Rivers; the cascading water creates one of the most vibrant and picturesque spots in the Garden State.

At the waters' juncture are two mills separated by a 200-foot waterfall. The Hunterdon Arts Center, housed in the Old Stone Mill, is across the 1870 iron bridge from the haunted Red Mill, (featured in the first volume of *Ghosts of the Garden State*).

Samuel Parry and his wife Selinda operated the old stone mill in the 19th century. Many are certain that Selinda's spirit stayed behind and along the way she has acquired the reputation as a "man-hating ghost."

In 1910, when all three floors of the mill collapsed, the cave-in was blamed on Selinda.

The gristmill was in operation until the 1950s but the spirit within the old place lay dormant for thirty years until the arts center set up shop and restored the fieldstone structure to its original appearance. The building now contains galleries, studios, *and* a strong supernatural presence.

During the mill's renovations in the 1980s, complaints of cold spots and baffling noises beleaguered the rehabilitation process.

7

Shadows darted furtively and disembodied footsteps resounded upstairs. Workmen refused to go into the stone mill alone, and others downright declined to return to the project when tools were flung at them from an unseen assailant. Some say it was Selinda perpetrating her punishment against the opposite sex.

Staff members heard doors slam throughout the building when they opened in the morning, yet the alarms never sounded and investigations failed to produce any human intruders.

Numerous psychics have visited the building and claimed contact with Selinda's spirit. But the clairvoyants could not uncover why the female phantom holds such a grudge against men.

Was Selinda a victim of abuse? Is this why she refuses to stay buried alongside her husband? We can only wonder. The secrets rest with the couple in Clinton's cemetery. The haunting engraving on their black marble tombstone eerily asks:

Why look ye here among the dead for the living?

OLDE COLUMBUS INNE
Columbus

The Olde Columbus Inne dates back to 1812 and the restaurant's haunted reputation is as long as its existence.

According to psychics, among the inn's ghostly patrons are a Native American who sits on his favorite barstool every now and then, and two female presences - an orphan who labored at the tavern in the early 19th century along with her abusive matronly co-worker.

A visit to the inn by members of South Jersey's Ghost Research team brought out the beast in a nasty being. While investigating the basement that was once a police barracks and jail, a researcher was suddenly gripped with a crushing headache. She felt as if her head was held in a vice. As her associates rushed to help her, they witnessed the nebulous form of a man and also caught his image on film. All the while, the group's dowsing rods were going wild.

The upstairs ladies' room is another gathering place for spirits; sightings are a common occurrence.

Photos snapped in a downstairs dining room revealed "orbs" of white light - the telltale sign of a phantom presence.

Henry Ludlam's descendants are living out a ghostly existence.

HENRY LUDLAM HOUSE
Dennisville

*H*enry Ludlam was a successful attorney and the first to organize the public school system in New Jersey. He was also a South Jersey real estate magnate; his considerable land holdings sprawled across the state from coast to coast.

In 1804, Ludlam erected a Federal style home on the shore of a 56-acre lake. Today his namesake pond on Route 47 honors the prosperous man.

There's more than meets the eye inside Ludlam's old house. From time to time the sound of shattering glass disturbs the peace in the antique home, yet no broken glass has ever been found. This baffling behavior is attributed to Ludlam's son Jonathan.

Jonathan Ludlam is a colorful character in the annals of Cape May County history. Described by some as a benevolent seaman, others allege he was a barbarous pirate to be avoided on the waters of Delaware Bay. He was at one time however, recognized for saving the crew of a floundering schooner.

Guests in the home have complained of chilly sensations and swear nocturnal spirits visited them in their room. One woman awoke in the middle of the night and spied a spectral child sitting on the edge of the bed staring at her.

The barely audible sound of a baby crying sometimes filters through the home although no infants live there.

Intuitives have deduced that at least two entities co-exist with the living inside the dwelling. Jonathan is described as a tall, bearded man who sits in his chair as if he was perched on a throne. The female phantom is Jonathan's wife Rachel. She continues to toil in the afterlife viewed in another dimension making candles.

Although the spirits like to keep themselves concealed they do dart about the house showing up as mercurial waves of energy.

Adding to the mystery of the home, many believe that Henry Ludlam's granddaughter was Edgar Allan Poe's inspiration for his lyric poem *Annabel Lee*.

ALLAIRE VILLAGE
Farmingdale

*A*t the restored village of Allaire, don't be surprised if you catch a glimpse of a misty, female apparition. The legendary lady in white roves across the quad from the General Store to the Big House. Who is this specter and why does she linger here? Psychics say she is the former admirer of Hal Allaire, the son of village founder James P. Allaire.

The property was known as Howell Furnace when Allaire purchased the bog-iron works in 1822 as a resource for his New York City foundry. (Allaire's Manhattan location manufactured the brass air chamber for Robert Fulton's steamboat the *Clermont*).

Allaire Village is unique in that the self-sufficient community created at the Howell Works included a church and a school. An entire town of over 400 people and 60 structures grew up around this industry that reached its peak around 1836.

Psychics focusing on this era discerned the residual energy of an extremely disagreeable man. They were able to detect that although he held an important position at the iron works he hated his job.

Village history records that a Benjamin Marks worked at Allaire in the second half of the 19th century.

The Visitors' Center in Allaire's row house is the most spiritually active spot in the park.

He held the position of Supervisor and would have lived in the row house. Allaire's row house was rebuilt on the remains of its original foundation and today the structure is home to the Visitors Center.

One Labor Day, staff members opened the Visitors Center and proceeded with their routine security check in the cellar. Their hearts were in their throats when they heard the sound of heavy footfalls down the hall only a few feet away.

As they cautiously approached the interloper they saw a sight that made their hair curl. The partial apparition of the lower half of a man stood before them in his boots and slowly faded from their sight.

The staff suspects this startling effect was the postmortem remains of the despised manager Benjamin Marks.

Other mystifying occurrences common in this section of the building are electrical anomalies. Lights, projectors, cameras and security systems usually go haywire for no explanation.

So - why does the lady in white stay behind endlessly walking the open square? Psychics say her story is that she ended her relationship with Hal Allaire in favor of another man. He was a sailor who went off to sea but never came back. Seems the hapless wraith keeps a fervent vigil still waiting for her man to return.

The wraith of a lonely widow still waits for her husband lost at sea inside the Lacey Township B.P.O.E.

LACEY TOWNSHIP ELKS CLUB
Forked River

Settled before the Revolution, early residents of the Village of Forked River keep their heads above water by fishing and shipbuilding. Some of the town's vintage structures still stand including the edifice housing the B.P.O.E. "Elks" Club on Beach Boulevard in the Forked River Beach section.

Originally, the century old house was a grand three story Victorian home owned by a ship captain and his wife. The Elks Club purchased the property in 1974 and a fire consumed the third floor in the 1980s.

Just about every member of the service club knows the sorrowful tale of "Isabelle," the name they've given to their resident ghost.

In days of yore, when men went off to sea, they left the women behind to tend the home. The wives waited patiently, and anxiously, hoping for a smooth voyage and their husband's safe return. Often times they left a candle or lamp burning in the window as a beacon for their loved one to find his way home.

But in this case, Isabelle's husband failed to return; she bravely faced her loss and lived out a lonely life in the big empty house.

Despite two new additions to the building, the interior is much as it was during Isabelle's tenancy.

Her spirit remains comfortable in the familiar surroundings where she spent so many years alone.

Recently a plumber who was working on the old home alleged he felt hands touching him as he worked in the basement.

Bartenders have felt the distinct presence of someone behind them and have heard the vague sound of someone calling out to them. They say the spirit is most likely the sea captain's wife.

On several occasions, after the bartenders have closed up shop and are driving home, they look back at the old place only to see that the lights are still on. Invariably, they turn around and drive back, unlock the door, and extinguish the light.

By the time they reach the parking lot, the lights are on again. Could this phenomenon be Isabelle's way of still burning a candle for husband out on the high seas?

Not surprisingly, Isabelle's apparition was sighted in the attic of the original building, the optimum vantage point to view her husband's long overdue vessel.

YELLOW FRAME CHURCH
Fredon

An ancient country church sits on the east side of NJ Route 94 at a crossroad six miles east of Blairstown. Oddly enough, the church's graveyard is in Frelinghuysen Township, Warren County, while the church stands across the road in Sussex County.

The following is excerpted from *A Genealogical Record of the Descendants of Nathan Armstrong:*

The First Presbyterian Church in the Hardwick Patent was organized at Hackettstown, where a log meetinghouse was erected about 1750. The Presbyterian families who had settled into the vicinity of Log Gaol attended this church, although it was ten miles away, but soon they felt strong enough to organize a separate congregation.

Accordingly, in 1763, they built a log meetinghouse at Dark Moon, but it was nine years later before they succeeded in securing the services of a regular pastor. This Church at Dark Moon was used as a place of Worship for more than 20 years before it was abandoned; in 1785 the congregation erected a new building at Shaw's Lane on the Ridge.

In 1841, the Yellow Frame was remodeled; in 1858, a vestibule and tower were built on the north end.... This Venerable house of worship is still standing, but it is no longer used for religious services; in 1887 a new edifice and a parsonage were erected on the opposite side of the road.

At the turn of the 19th century, as the new minister of Yellow Frame Church delivered his first sermon to the congregation he collapsed and died.

Originally buried in the Dark Moon graveyard across the street, the preacher was disinterred, for reasons unknown, and reburied in the Johnsonburg Cemetery. From that time, inexplicable phenomena plagued the holy place.

The most common anomaly was the sound of organ music emanating from the house of worship when no living soul was in sight.

A group of parishioners intent on getting to the bottom of the otherworldly music were welcomed by an invisible force that threw the heavy doors open to greet them. They were sure someone, or some*thing*, was inside watching them, yet they found no one.

Out of the blue, the rustling of the dry, fallen leaves outside caught their attention. The astonished group watched in awe as an indiscernible someone walked through the fallen foliage.

PIRATE JOHN'S HOUSE
Greenwich

*D*uring the 17th century, Greenwich was the official port of entry for all ships traveling on the Delaware River. Quaker John Fenwick laid out tree-lined Ye Greate Street in 1684 making the tidewater town in Cumberland County one of the oldest communities in southern New Jersey.

On the west side of Great Street is the Daniels house, which has engraved on its rainspout the date "1734." The house is said to contain the ghost of Pirate John, an 18th century buccaneer.

While tales of pirates and privateers (government licensed pirates) might sound fantastic, area historians confirm that the Delaware River and Bay suffered serious pirate problems and knew countless privateers in the first half of the 1700s.

A bandit, known only as Pirate John, betrayed his partners and turned "informant." The deceived cohorts tied John up in chains and left him to rot in the attic of the Daniel's house.

On stormy nights, believers claim you can still hear the rattle of Pirate John struggling with his chains in a futile attempt to free himself.

Pirate John stays behind rattling chains in the attic of the 1734 house nicknamed in his honor.

CENTENARY COLLEGE
Hackettstown

On the morning of April 9, 1886, newspapers headlines announced that the battered remains of an 18-year-old were found in a field behind Centenary Collegiate Institute.

Matilda Smith, employed as live-in kitchen help, had been murdered the night before after attending a performance at Hackettstown's Main Street assembly hall. Because "Tillie" expected to return after the ten o'clock curfew, she discussed with janitor James Titus the possibility of his letting her in if she were locked out.

The physical evidence, paint and wood chips found on the body, indicated that the crime had been committed indoors and the corpse moved to the spot where it was found. The cause of death was by strangulation during an attempted rape.

James Titus, 29, who was initially sentenced to the gallows after being convicted of the rape and murder, asserted that he had accidentally killed Tillie in a fit of rage after a tryst.

After he had served 19 years in prison, Titus' death sentence was commuted. He died at age 95 in 1952.

Tillie was buried in a pauper's grave but because she became a symbol of feminine virtue, a movement was begun to construct a memorial in her honor.

Photo credit: Find-A-Grave.com

Contributions poured in to town officials and an elaborate white marble monument was erected in Union Cemetery in her memory. A graceful classical figure, holding a wreath, ornaments the tombstone that bears the inscription: *She died in defence of her honor.*

For over a hundred years, students at the Institute, now Centenary College, have shared tales of the poor country girl's ghost at the school. Tillie's spirit, which reportedly materializes on occasion, is most often discerned walking dormitory halls. When Tillie's spirit is on the prowl, particularly on the third floor of the South dormitory, (supposedly where Tillie resided) flickering lights are a revealing sign of her ghostly presence.

Photo credit: Find-A-Grave.com

The spirit of Tillie Smith stays alive watching out for the female students at Centenary College.

SOURLAND MOUNTAIN PRESERVE
Hillsborough

Steeped in history, the Sourland region is rife with tales of the supernatural. When hiker's compass needles spin wildly, the problem is blamed on "Black Betty."

Elizabeth Wert was a young patriot who met with a gruesome death for the part she played in the War for Independence. Commonly known as Betty, her fiancé left New Jersey to fight for the cause in New England. Every day, without fail, Betty sat knitting on a promontory in the Sourland hills whiling away the time and waiting for her beloved to return. He never would.

Eventually, knitting Betty took a more active role in our country's struggle and agreed to spy for the Continental Army. From her outpost she had a bird's eye view of British maneuvers in the Raritan Valley. History records that her surveillance was vital to the colonist's victory at the Battle of Monmouth.

Unfortunately, the enemy discovered Betty's espionage and the young woman was captured, endured the horrors of prison life, and was executed by decapitation in 1778.

For centuries thereafter, Betty's ghost was reported traipsing about the glacial boulders and knitting away on rocks and roadsides.

Author Michael Haynes, claims to have seen "a

stunning brunette in a long blue dress" sitting on a rock overlooking the Watchung Mountain Range in 1989. Twenty-three years old at the time, he knew nothing about the legend of Black Beauty of the Sourlands. Haynes was so struck by the woman's good looks that he stopped his car and got out to introduce himself. When he did so, the beauty vanished.

Moved by the experience, he researched the region's history and told the story of one of Black Betty's sordid post mortem escapades in *WEIRD NJ* magazine.

In the 1920s, the Rock Creek postmaster's chicken coop was raided for weeks and many fowls were slaughtered. This trespassing was a serious offense. Finally, one night when the postmaster heard his poultry's frenzy, he immediately reached for his shotgun, ran out, and fired. The culprit lay dead in a heap.

As he held his lantern aloft, he realized that he had made a terrible mistake - he had killed his wife.

The bereft man brought the woman's body into the house and called the sheriff. When the lawman arrived he found the postmaster's wife propped in a kitchen chair with a huge hole in her chest. Next to her sat her husband - his head severed and nowhere to be found.

Immediately after the unforgettable episode, sightings of Betty increased dramatically. All were sure that this was Betty's way to inform the public that she had finally exacted revenge for her untimely death.

LITTLE DEBBIE'S GRAVE
Imlaystown

Samuel Lincoln and Hannah Salter, daughter of wealthy New Jersey mill owner Richard Salter, were the great-grandparents of President Abraham Lincoln. The ruins of their blacksmith shop still stand on a back road in Cream Ridge.

In 1717, they gave birth to a baby girl they named Deborah. Children's mortality rates were high in the 18th century and the little girl died when she was only three years old.

Lincoln's great-aunt is buried in Monmouth County's Ye Olde Robbins Burial Place. If you're willing to brave the tick infested thicket surrounding the iron barred plot, you may experience the haunting activity associated with the gravesite.

The death of a child is never easy and some say the sadness endured by the Lincoln family still lingers at her grave. Over the years locals reported that during May, the month when the young girl died, gut-wrenching sobs would be heard and the eerie sight of a horse-drawn funeral cortege shrouded in haze was seen entering the tiny cemetery.

THE PAULINSKILL VIADUCT
Knowlton

When the Paulinskill Viaduct was constructed in 1909, the train trestle was considered one of the "Wonders of the World." The Lackawanna Railroad erected the arched 115-foot high concrete bridge that spans 1,100 feet across the Paulinskill River.

Tragedy marred the building of this modern marvel when a construction worker was buried alive as the cement was poured. A ghostly legend grew from the disaster and there are those who say the dutiful worker is on overtime in the afterlife. His apparition is said to walk the trestle inspecting his crewmates handiwork.

The abandoned viaduct was one of New Jersey's hidden treasures until the state acquired the property in 1985 and transformed the land into a state park.

Paulinskill Viaduct and its environs is a "must see" - you might just get a peek of the tireless worker whose shift is eternal.

COKESBURY INN
Lebanon

The Cokesbury Inn began its days as a stopover on the stagecoach line from New Brunswick, NJ to Easton, PA in 1836. Travelers supped on hearty meals downstairs and slept in their rented room upstairs.

Today the owners and their staff are comfortable with the friendly spirits that linger in the vintage wooden structure.

Workers have encountered several different nebulous spirits on the basement stairs and in the upstairs bedrooms and halls. A former chef, who was temporarily lodged in one of the rooms, claimed that she received nightly visits from a 6-year-old specter.

A clairvoyant perceived the young ghost, named Veronica, lived upstairs with her mother who worked as a cook at the Cokesbury. According to the psychic, the little girl died from the Spanish flu in 1918. Apparently Veronica was unaware of her own passing and the reason her spirit lingered was because she was trying to find her mom.

The sensitive helped the girl's spirit release its hold on the mortal world and cross over to the other side.

Another eerie episode occurred one afternoon near the bar. Two workers heard the back door open and close. Then, through a stained glass wall, they saw a person's shadow pass on its way to the bathroom. They scampered to see who had come in, found no one, but were keenly aware of the distinct lavender scent the shade left behind.

The mysterious sweet-smelling spirit turns out to be Lydia Huffman, the inn's first housekeeper. Lydia loved her job and her habit was to arrive early every day, clean the sheets, and make lavender soap.

Every couple of weeks, the sound of a man running down the stairs plagues the place. A local ghost buster deduced that the sound was "an impression upon the atmosphere." The unseen male causing the commotion was a boarder who, when he witnessed a gas explosion across the street that killed ten people, raced down the stairs to help out. His spirit remains frozen in time reenacting the incident over and over.

Others spirits served up at the inn include a giggling girl who cowers in a corner and a bereft woman who paces the upstairs hall.

The Cokesbury Inn was also a stop on the Underground Railroad and a forbidding room in the basement was a hideout on the freedom trail. Workers feel a palpable resistance when they descend the stairs to get supplies from the cellar. The ice-cold energy force has even compelled some workers to quit.

The spirits at the Cokesbury Inn aren't mean or vindictive and those who stay employed there are like Lydia Huffman; they love their job and have grown accustomed to their otherworldly associates.

A devoted teacher keeps the fire burning at the Little Red School House.

LITTLE RED SCHOOL HOUSE
Lyndhurst

*I*n 1804, Jacob Van Winkle presented a strip of land to town trustees for the construction of a school. The annual rent was one peppercorn, "if demanded."

The county erected a one-room schoolhouse and the public school system began. In 1893, the present school was built and used for classes until 1980.

In 1984 the Township purchased the school and leased the historic relic to the Lyndhurst Historical Society in order to preserve this unique landmark.

The Little Red Schoolhouse Museum, at 400 Riverside Avenue, focuses on local history and contains a circa 1912 schoolroom, artifacts and memorabilia - and some say a ghost.

In the past, some observers witnessed the apparition of a woman dressed in an antique white blouse and a long, beige skirt. At times the teacher's specter manifested as a full-bodied apparition while at other times she appeared in transparent form.

When the light-haired phantom revealed herself, she seemed to be lost in her own world as she gathered firewood in her arms. Her movements indicated that she was placing the invisible logs in the pot-bellied stove and then gave the impression of lighting a fire.

*The Abbott House Inn where the tormented spirit
of a young boy still roams.*

ABBOTT HOUSE INN
Mays Landing

At the head of the Great Egg Harbor River is the Atlantic County seat of Mays Landing. Founded by Philadelphia trader George May in 1760, the town's historic district boasts over 250 buildings.

The Abbott House Inn is a Victorian mansion built in the 1860s by prominent attorney Joseph E. P. Abbott and his wife Adeline.

The resident ghost is a 16-year-old boy named David. Psychics explain the haunting is due to the boy's trauma of being locked inside a closet when he was alive. As a consequence of this cruel punishment, his spirit remains trapped where he experienced intense emotional upset.

Sometimes David will appear to children. When he prefers to remain invisible, the opening and closing of doors is attributed to the young man moving about the house.

ACORN HALL
Morristown

Named for one of the largest and oldest red oak trees in New Jersey, Acorn Hall is an 1853 Italianate mansion. Home to the Morris County Historical Society, the Victorian house museum is unique in that it retains most of its original furnishings.

The preserved environment is the perfect setting for an attractive ghost, who feels right at home in the familiar surroundings. The specter is the young widow of the home's first owner, Dr. John Schermerhorn.

Remarkably, her full-bodied apparition slowly walking down the main staircase is the most frequent paranormal phenomenon. Witnesses who have seen widow Schermerhorn's ghost describe her wearing a taffeta dress, bonnet, and carrying a wicker basket on her arm. The distinct sounds of footsteps and a crinkling skirt accompany her appearance. Perhaps she is on her way outside to gather flowers from the authentic gardens.

Another uncanny occurrence at the historic home is the sound of a porch swing rhythmically swaying back and forth. Strangely, there is no porch swing at Acorn Hall.

THOMAS BUDD HOUSE
Mount Holly

The Thomas Budd House is the earliest known residence on its original site in Mount Holly. Budd was a plantation owner who built his house on White Street in 1744. The historic home functioned for a while as a museum but is now private residences with retail stores on the lower floors.

The proprietor of a first floor gift shop sensed an angry and aggressive presence in the basement and felt him staring at her. His shadowy figure was spotted passing by a side window.

Spectral men wearing tri-cornered hats have been seen in the stores and restaurant.

Psychics were able to identify that the dominant presence who still resides in the ancient stone home is an early 19th century caretaker. The sensitive described him with long, straggly, gray hair, blue eyes and bad teeth; he was perceived lighting lamps and carrying a ring of keys.

Despite his unseemly appearance he despises clutter, desires cleanliness and order, and prefers the stillness of the basement - he cannot tolerate all the activity upstairs.

Another entity abides in the house. She is the spirit of a melancholy 18th century woman who wears her hair pulled back and parted in the middle. Her story remains an unsolved mystery.

The Thomas Budd House maintains the spirit of a finicky caretaker.

RITZ THEATER
Oaklyn

*T*he vintage marquee beckons one to enter the Ritz and step back in time to an earlier era...

Original canvas wall murals adorn lobby walls and tuxedoed ushers greet the evening theater crowd. The landmark showplace welcomes *all* - dead or alive.

Bruce A. Corliss rescued the stately old 471-seat theatre in 1985 and the "Puttin' on the Ritz" theater group moved right in.

The theatre originally opened as a vaudeville house in 1927. When the vaudeville circuit came to a close in the 1940s, the Ritz exclusively showed first-run movies. Many locals have fond memories of watching James Dean in *Rebel Without a Cause* in the 1950s. The theater's downturn came in the 1970s, when pornographic movies took center stage.

The well-preserved showhouse provides a theatrical setting for its ghostly populace.

In addition to the motion detector being tripped for no reason, some of the more dramatic paranormal anomalies experienced by the acting troupe are the sound of audible breathing, the sight of a tall specter walking down the hall, the appearance of figures on stage, a disembodied hand on an auditorium seat, and

Ghosts are still puttin' on the Ritz at this Oaklyn theater.

the apparition of a short, mustachioed man with an upturned nose sitting in the audience.

South Jersey Ghost Researchers (SJGR) responded to the call for extra help in sorting out the resident phantoms. SJGR investigators spent numerous nights exploring the theater's inexplicable performances.

The mission of most ghost hunting groups is to provide documentation of the existence of spirits as evidence that life continues beyond death. This is most often achieved through photography because cameras don't filter out everything like our eyes and minds do. The most common ways spirits are captured on film or videotape are orbs of light, ectoplasm (whitish mist), or a column of light called a vortex.

SJGR used digital and video cameras when shadows and silhouettes were perceived at the Ritz. They focused on the vacant audience seating, orchestra pit, stage, and projection room. Not surprisingly, the photos and video displayed orbs and in some cases, white nebulous forms.

In fact, the theater is so spiritually active that the SJGR group now auditions its prospective members at the haunted playhouse.

Attendance at the popular vintage theater is a must; the sideshows are out of this world.

FLANDERS HOTEL
Ocean City

A life-sized portrait of "Emily, the Lady in White" adorns the marble foyer of the vintage Flanders Hotel.

For decades, the long departed spirit, affectionately called "Emily," has been haunting the guesthouse startling all who encounter her ethereal form. Even children have claimed to talk to the pretty woman who shares "secrets" with them and then mysteriously disappears down a dark hallway.

According to legend, the unearthly Emily is said to have been the fiancé of a World War I soldier who never returned from battle. Years ago, when a wedding photograph was snapped inside the hotel, Emily's ghostly image developed in the photo.

Other unexplained occurrences attributed to her presence are the sounds of disembodied footsteps echoing in the lobby and the inexplicable locking of certain hotel doors.

GARRETT MOUNTAIN RESERVATION
Paterson

The 77-foot high Great Falls of the Passaic River is a national landmark and was an 18th century tourist attraction. Even George Washington, the Marquis de Lafayette, and Alexander Hamilton were awestruck when they stopped to eat lunch at the site during a break in the Revolution.

Visitors from New York City traveled three days to catch a glimpse of the natural wonder. Sometimes an added attraction was the astonishing sight of a specter emerging from the mist thought to be the ghost of someone who committed suicide at the falls.

The visionary Hamilton saw beyond the cascade's beauty to its awesome power and sought to harness its energy for the development of industry vital to establishing the fledgling country's economy. Twelve years later, as Secretary of the Treasury, he planned the city's industrialization.

In 1791, the area surrounding the falls was named Paterson after the then governor and signer of the Declaration of Independence, William Paterson.

By the 1840s, Paterson was nicknamed "Silk City" because every phase of silk production took place in the flourishing city except for the raising of the silkworms.

Catholina Lambert was one of the industry's leaders and he erected a pretentious stone mansion known today as Lambert's Castle. The house has undergone extensive renovation and the Passaic County Historical Society operates the historic dwelling as a museum.

Lambert Castle is located in the Garret Mountain Reservation, a county park with open fields, fishing pond, overlook and picnic areas. Garret Mountain is also a national natural landmark because of its uncommon variety of rare minerals resulting from the volcanic activity responsible for its creation. The park is also a good place to look for hawks - and ghosts.

Long before the property was home to the Paterson silk baron, the grounds held a military encampment. It appears that a Revolutionary War revenant still stands guard.

According to those who witnessed his apparition when leaving the park at closing, a transparent figure dressed in a colonial uniform limps along the roadway holding his injured arm.

PROPRIETARY HOUSE
Perth Amboy

In 1683, William Penn and eleven other men, the Proprietors of East New Jersey, purchased the East Jersey tract from the estate of Sir George Carteret. Perth Amboy served as the capital of East Jersey, one of twin capitals, until 1702.

The Proprietary House is the country's only remaining royal governor's house. Built in 1764, the brick Georgian mansion was erected on 11 acres for His Excellency William Franklin, Governor of the Province of New Jersey and the son of Benjamin Franklin.

In 1775, the elder Franklin journeyed to Perth Amboy to persuade his son to withdraw his allegiance from Britain. Although the elder statesman pleaded, ranted and raved, William would not be swayed. Benjamin grieved over his failure to show William the error of his ways, and later wrote to a friend, "I am deserted by my only son."

Governor William Franklin was arrested in 1776 for supporting the British.

After the Revolution, the interior was destroyed by fire, but later restored, enlarged, and established as the Brighton House. For a few years, the hotel flourished catering to the rich and fashionable, but its popularity dwindled at the outbreak of the War of 1812.

45

Years later, Matthias Bruen delighted in his ownership and orchestrated gala parties. After he gave up the ghost, so to speak, something extraordinary occurred.

Legend says that promptly at twelve o'clock the wheels of a coach would resonate up the driveway. Sycamore trees bent and groaned, dogs howled, doors of every room creaked, and the home's heavy front portal flew open to greet its ghostly master.

Dr. Alexander M. Bruen bequeathed the palace to the Presbyterian Church in 1883. For fifty years, the house was home to disabled Presbyterian clergymen and their families.

The Proprietary House Association has been restoring the historic structure since 1966. Although it has lost much of its grand appearance, it is still a palace, and continues to interest fans of old Perth Town.

Locals assert the place remains haunted by the specter of a little boy whose visage is sometimes seen staring out the windows.

PRINCETON UNIVERSITY
Princeton

*R*ightfully so, Princeton University is exceedingly proud of the role it played in the American Revolution.

Built in 1756, Nassau Hall was once the largest building in the country and housed the entire college. The edifice was home to the Continental Congress when Princeton was the capital of the country during the later half of 1783.

The sturdy stone structure survived bombardment during the American Revolution, (a cannonball scar is visible on an exterior wall), occupation by troops of both sides during the war, and two fires. In 1777, General George Washington forced the British out of Nassau Hall.

Revolutionary War ghosts purportedly haunt the venerable edifice and another of Princeton's legendary ghosts is that of a dying British soldier, who is oftentimes sighted in the basement of Holder Hall.

But a more contemporary spirit is found at the building that houses a student theater group and bears his name - Hamilton Murray Hall.

Princeton graduate Hamilton Murray set sail for France in 1872, the year after his commencement. Tragically, the promising young man perished when his ship was lost at sea.

47

The haunting portrait of a glowing Princeton alumnus.

In 1879, Murray's family commissioned a new campus building in Hamilton's memory.

For years, students have reported unexplainable phenomena and the feeling of a definite presence in the vaulted space where a large portrait of Hamilton is the focal point of the room. Some students who have fallen asleep near the painting in the cozy alcove, awake to the sight of Murray's glowing image shining brightly in the dark room.

The stage, however, is epicenter of more inexplicable events. Objects move of their own accord; most often scenery sets and tools disappear and then reappear in other areas of the stage.

The most stunning manifestation witnessed by numerous students over the years is that during dress rehearsals a young man dressed in a long coat and top hat is sighted sitting in a row to the left of the stage intently watching the performance.

49

WOODNUTT COUNTRY INN
Salem

*I*n 1675, a group of Quakers settled on the banks of the Delaware River and named their community Salem, meaning "shalom" (peace). Salem was the first permanent settlement in West New Jersey.

The Woodnutt Country Inn is only one of many restored buildings in the historic town. During the day, owner Donna Robinson manages the bed and breakfast inn and her silent, and not so invisible partner, Sarah the ghost, works the night shift.

Sarah, who was previously employed as a lace maker, lived in the house and died in 1889. She may have died, but some feel she has never left.

Robinson discovered she was co-habitating with a female phantom in 1992. A 29-year-old male guest told her that while he was lying in bed he saw the shadow of a woman. Other men who claim to have seen Sarah's specter relate that the spirit wears a long white gown. Even Robinson's son has received nocturnal visits.

At the time of her death, Sarah was only 33 and still unmarried. So far, her harmless appearances have been to men who are about her own age.

Robinson wants to assure prospective visitors, however, of a *gently* spirited stay in the peaceful B & B.

FORT HANCOCK
Sandy Hook

Since the American Revolution, Sandy Hook has been a strategic site for defense and navigation. Numerous fortifications have stood at the north end of the six-mile peninsula to protect the New York Harbor.

In 1899, Fort Hancock was established and thirty-four buildings were erected, including the elegant row of Georgian Revival style officers' homes that still stand sentry at the water's edge.

Fort Hancock was outfitted with the most sophisticated weaponry of the period. In 1893 Battery Potter was completed, featuring the nation's first and only steam-lift gun battery.

A wide variety of weapons were employed at Fort Hancock from cannons to Nike missiles. Until the weapons became too powerful, Sandy Hook also served as a proving ground.

Even though many of the gun emplacements and structures have fallen into disrepair, a tour of the complex provides an enlightening experience and can elicit a ghost story or two.

A volunteer guide offered that after he had made up a bed in the old barracks, Building 102, an impression appeared as if someone had lain there. He smoothed the bed again, and left the room.

A spectral soldier clutching a rifle once stood guard on the steps of the house now occupied by the New Jersey Audubon Society.

When he returned, only moments later, the indentation was back on the bed and no one else had entered the room.

When the unpaid helper shared this incident with others, they had had the same experience. The volunteers concurred that the bed-ridden revenant could possibly be an ordnance accident victim from an earlier day at the experimental weapons facility.

"History House" is a restored home on Officer's Row and is open to the public. A visitor on tour of the house declared that she had lived in the dwelling next door - to the right of History House. An officer had committed suicide by hanging himself inside that home and the woman claimed that his ghost appeared to her regularly when she lived there as a child.

Previous families had been driven out by the dead man's specter she asserted. Some prior tenants alleged they had witnessed his floating head covered with blood, while others attested that a pair of disembodied shoes walked up the stairs.

Since the ghost liked the woman's family he toned down his scary antics and allowed them to stay.

For many years, the specter of a soldier with rifle in hand was sighted standing guard on the porch of Building 20. The New Jersey Audubon Society now occupies the structure and reports no haunting activity.

53

The classic Essex Sussex where some guests still refuse to leave.

THE ESSEX SUSSEX HOUSE
Spring Lake

*T*he Essex and Sussex was once a grand seaside hotel - a magical place amid wind-swept beaches and a beautiful spring-fed lake. Opened in 1920, for decades thereafter the hotel reigned as the crown jewel of the Jersey Shore attracting royalty, presidents, and high society. Today the edifice is a luxury oceanfront residence for adults.

When the massive building stood vacant, a lone watchman was responsible to make sure the building was secure to ward off trespassing. There were times, in the dead of the night, when the caretaker discerned the din of revelers in the ballroom. Music, laughter, the clamor of people eating, drinking and partying filtered through the cavernous structure. When the caretaker reached the room and opened the door the noise stopped and the room was empty.

Workmen renovating the building's interior for condominiums in 1982 experienced the uncomfortable feeling of being watched. They were certain to avoid working on the fifth floor because there they glimpsed a dark shadow peering at them from the end of the extensive hallway. When they tried to see who was peering at them, the furtive shade darted out of sight.

A misty apparition appeared in the Ocean County Courthouse.

OCEAN COUNTY COURTHOUSE
Toms River

*T*he new governing body of Ocean County conducted their organizational meeting in May 1850 at the tavern of Thomas P. Barkalow, located on the corner of Main and Water Streets in Toms River. Toms River became the county seat by one vote over Lakehurst.

The design of the Greek revival style Courthouse is the temple form that was popular during the mid-19th century. The new Courthouse was built with bricks shipped by schooners from Haverstraw, New York and unloaded at Robbins Cove at the foot of Allen Street. Teams of horses pulled wagonloads of the blocks up the hill to the construction site on an old cornfield.

In 1994, Courtroom I was besieged by a series of strange occurrences. Doors knobs rattled, motion detectors went off inside empty rooms, and lights blinked on and off for no reason.

The misty apparition of a middle-aged man smartly dressed in a shirt and tie revealed himself inside the courtroom along with a tear-shaped filmy figure.

THE COLLEGE OF NEW JERSEY
Trenton

One of the ghosts at the College of New Jersey, formerly Trenton State College, is thought to be a young woman murdered over Labor Day weekend in 1977. Her naked body was found wrapped in a piano cover on the stage in Kendall Hall.

A psychic medium claimed the piano major was the victim of a stalker.

To this day, her murderer walks free. To this day, the victim prowls the campus bound to the place where she died. She also gets blamed for the many mysterious, unsolved incidents at the school.

Students sometimes feel they are being "watched" and experience unexplainable cold spots. Doors, much too heavy for the wind to blow, slam shut of their own accord.

Haunting strains of piano music filter through the atmosphere late at night when Kendall Hall is locked up tight and no living soul occupies the music building.

Possibly this is the victim's way to remind us that her killer remains on the prowl.

SHADES OF DEATH ROAD
Warren County

*S*hades of Death Road passes through Liberty, Independence and Allamuchy Townships. The renowned road skirts the muck lands of the Great Meadows - the ancient bed of a glacial lake that now nourishes sod and truck farms with its rich black soil. The five-mile long road continues through countryside bordered by boulders, canyons and hillside caves, once inhabited by Native Americans.

In the late 1940s William Crouse Jr. and Leon G. Hull erected splendid homes in the deep woods. The two neighbors built a dam across a small stream that ran through their properties, which thereby created quite a large lake. They named their new lake "Ghost Lake" for the ghost-like wisps of fog that rose from the water.

The ominous sounding road winds along Ghost Lake and presents a lovely country drive. The road is framed by towering trees and was originally called "Shades Road."

Once a stagecoach route, the isolated location was a prime spot for thievery and murder. Wildcats found the ledges prime lookouts for hunting and, according to some, attacking humans. Crouse and Hull named the surrounding mountain "Murderers Mountain" and their property "Haunted Hollow."

Great Meadows swamp was at one time infested with millions of mosquitoes supposedly responsible for spreading malaria among Native Americans encamped near the Shades.

The aggressive Iroquois provoked the peaceful Lenni Lenape and stealthily approached the tribe via the Delaware Water Gap. The New York natives slaughtered large numbers of Lenape. Tribesmen claimed to see the wispy spirits of their fallen comrades in the heavy fog that often hung over the valley.

Ultimately the Shades Road came to be known as the Shades of *Death* Road.

Prior to the Civil War, an itinerant peddler and his horse were found dead on the roadway. The mysterious death was certain robbery but the murderer was never apprehended.

In the 1930s, another robbery victim was slain in his Model T Ford. He had been bludgeoned to death with the jack handle from his car. His perpetrator was never found.

To this day, strange, mesmerizing pillars of mist, known as the Great Meadows Fog, rise over the water and capture the imagination of many a traveler. Some are taken aback when the cloudy columns take on human form and navigate their way along the lonely country road.

DEY MANSION
Wayne

With the British occupying New York City, General George Washington encamped his army in the strategic Preakness Valley and established his headquarters at the Dey Mansion from July 1 to July 29, 1780.

The stately Georgian manor house was built in the 1740s by Dirck Dey, whose son, Theunis, went on to become a Colonel of the Bergen County Militia during the Revolutionary War.

Washington was not the only famous personage to pass through the portals of the stately home - Alexander Hamilton, Marquis de Lafayette, Lord Stirling, and "Mad" Anthony Wayne, stopped in, to name a few.

Today the house is owned and operated as a museum by Passaic County. The two-acre site includes several replica outbuildings, including a Blacksmith Shop and Plantation House

Guided tours transport the visitor to an earlier era that marks a momentous time in our country's history.

Is the Dey Mansion haunted? Just about any aged house involved in the onerous effort to form a nation holds the residual energy of that intense struggle.

Staff members admit to a presence that manifests as "a gentle breeze that caresses their shoulders."

General George Washington headquartered at the Dey Mansion
where a subtle and soothing presence pervades the historic house.

GUGGENHEIM LIBRARY
West Long Branch

Monmouth University's 138-acre campus is situated on two former grand estates. Woodrow Wilson Hall, formerly Shadow Lawn, is a 128-room limestone mansion modeled on Versailles. The national landmark structure was built on the site of the former president's summer home that burned.

Across Cedar Avenue from Shadow Lawn is the Murry and Leonie Guggenheim Library built where the state's only vice-president, Garret A. Hobart, once lived.

In 1903, Guggenheim appointed the New York firm of M. Carrere and Thomas Hastings to design his summer cottage.

The Beaux Arts building, completed in 1905, was intended exclusively for summer use. The lofty interior and floor-to-ceiling doors and windows allowed summer breezes to cool the rooms. The architects received the gold medal from the American Institute of Architects for the design. (Carrere and Hastings also designed the New York Public Library at Fifth Avenue & 42nd Street in New York City.)

Murry Guggenheim died in 1939 but Leonie continued to summer at her West Long Branch mansion until she passed away twenty years later.

An inconspicuous spirit is among the stacks at Monmouth University's Guggenheim Library.

Many detect a definite presence in the library's atmosphere. A perceptive French student shared with a librarian that she was distracted from her studies because she was certain someone was watching her.

Around Halloween, the library conducts "ghost" tours. Visitors are awestruck when they reach the back stairs and notice the perceptible drop in temperature. Another spooky manifestation in that area is that an invisible someone causes the stairs to creak.

The computer room is located in a space that was once a bathroom. Several anomalies disturb this spot.

Cursors move on computer screens when no operators are near the monitors; sometimes inexplicable tiny triangles show up on the screens. Technical types can't fathom this phantom behavior.

From time to time, the smell of perfume is noticeable even though none of the workers wear cologne.

One unforgettable incident was when the office door slammed really hard. "It couldn't have been the wind because the window is permanently closed," offered one source. There remains no explanation for the strange occurrence.

GLOUCESTER COUNTY COURTHOUSE
Woodbury

On Friday nights between the hours of 10 P.M. and midnight, you'll find the specter of John "Jumping Jack" Craddock floating down the stairs, through the halls, and back up to his jail cell.

Craddock was an inmate who was imprisoned for burglary but unable to post bail. He hanged himself in his 6 by 8 foot cell around 10 P.M. in December 1982.

The ghost of the Pennsauken man made his otherworldly debut when construction workers were renovating the old Gloucester County Courthouse several years ago. They nicknamed him "Sparky" because Craddock's wraith was first noticed through the sparks caused by the workers as they dismantled the steel barred prison cells.

Before the renovations, the prison was dank and gloomy and described as a "hellhole." The lockup was so spooky that Hollywood studios had approached county officials wanting to film a movie there.

One of the 63 cells was saved and preserved for posterity. As it turns out that is the cell were Sparky is forever confined. To this day, night workers routinely see his specter roaming through the courthouse.

GULLY ROAD
Woodside

One of America's most haunted roads was located in New Jersey in the vicinity of Woodside, a beautiful village with wide tree-lined streets located along the Passaic River.

The well-worn path was the result of erosion from water run off that created a gully after which the road was named. Gully Road appeared on the town's earliest maps and was used by the town's earliest settlers. Even before the onslaught of immigration the Lenni Lenape tribe used the gully as a path to the river.

Due to urbanization, most of Gully Road has been obliterated and obscured by Route 21 and the Erie-Lackawanna Railroad tracks, but a section of the ancient street still exists and is known as Herbert Place.

Gully Road was always considered haunted probably because the pre-historic path lay below the earth line and only the bravest dared to walk through the ditch at night. An elderly couple lived on the lane at the junction of Gully Road and Washington Avenue (now Broadway). When the town fathers determined that the road needed to be widened for clear passage of wagons to the river, the couple refused to vacate their home and stubbornly rejected relocating.

Some townspeople became impatient with the old folks and organized a troupe of irate citizens who literally tore the house down one evening with the helpless inhabitants inside.

Even though the couple expired they never left the neighborhood. They were often seen wandering Gully Road and seemed to be searching for their lost abode.

The ghostly pair walked together with another unearthly spirit, the specter of a British spy.

Legend has it that a Tory was caught spying on the ships in the river during the Revolutionary War. Captured by the patriots, the loyalist was tried on the spot and immediately hung from a large tree at the bend in the road.

A trickster in life, the soldier continued his antics from beyond the grave, for he was known to play pranks on anyone who crossed his path near Gully Road.

ACKNOWLEDGEMENTS

The author wants to recognize and thank the following individuals for their contributions to this book:

Bruce Corliss
Ritz Theater

Sandy Epstein
Murry and Leonie Guggenheim Library

Robert François
Cumberland County Historical Society

Dawn Hartpence

James N. Hogan
Gloucester County Clerk

Liv Ingrid Kristoffersen

Tom Lenz

Arlene Potenzone
Dey Mansion

Brian & Katie Weir

A special thank you to the friendly and courteous staff of Sheridan Books for their professional printing; of special note: Crystal Brinson, Debra Tremper, and Rebecca Humrich.

RESOURCES

Abrams, Sheila, "Tillie Smith: A Hackettstown story." *The Star Gazette,* May 4, 1989.

Beck, Henry Charlton: *Tales And Towns Of Northern New Jersey.* New Brunswick, N.J., Rutgers University Press, 1964.

_____, *More Forgotten Towns of Southern New Jersey.* Rutgers University Press, New Brunswick, NJ; 1963

Conte, Stephen, "Lincoln's New Jersey Roots." *WEIRD NJ,* Issue #13, Bloomfield, NJ; 1999.

Hauck, Dennis William, *Haunted Places, The National Directory.* Penguin Press, New York, NY; 1996.

Haynes, Michael, "Beware the Wrath of Black Betty of the Sourland Mountains." *WEIRD NJ,* Issue#13, Bloomfield, NJ; 1999.

Heckman, Candace, "A hanged inmate, a haunted courthouse. *The Philadelphia Inquirer,* Philadelphia, PA.

Holzer, Hans, *Travel Guide to Haunted Places.* Black Dog & Levanthal Publishers, New York, NY; 1993.

Jaccarino, Mike, "Lacey Elks Club has one particularly spirited soul." *Press of Atlantic City,* Atlantic, City, NJ; October 31, 2002.

Kerry, "The Ghost of the Little Red School House." *WEIRD NJ,* Issue #17, Bloomfield, NJ.

Roberts, Russell and Richard Youmans, *Down the Jersey Shore.* Rutgers University Press, New Brunswick, NJ; 1993.

Sickler, Joseph S., *Tea Burning Town.* The Greenwich Press, Bridgeton, NJ.

Siebold, David J. & Adams, Charles J. III, *Cape May Ghost Stories.* Exeter House Books, Barnegat Light, NJ & Reading, PA; 1988.

"Strange Occurrences At Garrett Mountain," *WEIRD NJ,* Issue #9, Bloomfield. NJ.

Suwa, C. Keiko, "The Real Deal on the Trenton State Ghost" *WEIRD NJ,* Issue #16, Bloomfield, NJ.

Weinstein, Sheryl, "Favorite haunts." *The Star Ledger,* Newark, NJ; October 27, 1999.

Westergaard, Barbara, *New Jersey, A Guide to the State, 2nd Edition."* Rutgers University Press, New Brunswick, NJ; 1998.

Wright, James, "Grim folklore spawned on Shades of Death Road." *The Express-Times,* NJ; May 2, 1993.

WEBSITES:

Are We There Yet?
www.fieldtrip.com/nj

FOXNews.com

Haunted New Jersey
www.hauntednj.com

New Jersey History's Mysteries
www.njhm.com

New Jersey Online
www.nj.com

The Press of Atlantic City
www.pressplus.com

South Jersey Ghost Research
www.sjgr.org

Sandy Hook peninsula swarms with spirits from earlier days.

The author is always
looking for
true ghost stories.
If you have one
you'd like to share
please contact:

BLACK CAT PRESS
Post Office Box 1218
Forked River, NJ 08731
or
e-mail:
llmacken@hotmail.com

Thanks.

LOOK FOR THESE OTHER TITLES BY:

Lynda Lee Macken

HAUNTED CAPE MAY
GHOSTS OF THE GARDEN STATE
GHOSTLY GOTHAM – NEW YORK CITY'S
HAUNTED HISTORY
HAUNTED HISTORY OF STATEN ISLAND
ADIRONDACK GHOSTS
HAUNTED SALEM & BEYOND
ADIRONDACK GHOSTS II

For purchasing information contact:

BLACK CAT PRESS
Post Office Box 1218
Forked River, New Jersey 08731

llmacken@hotmail.com